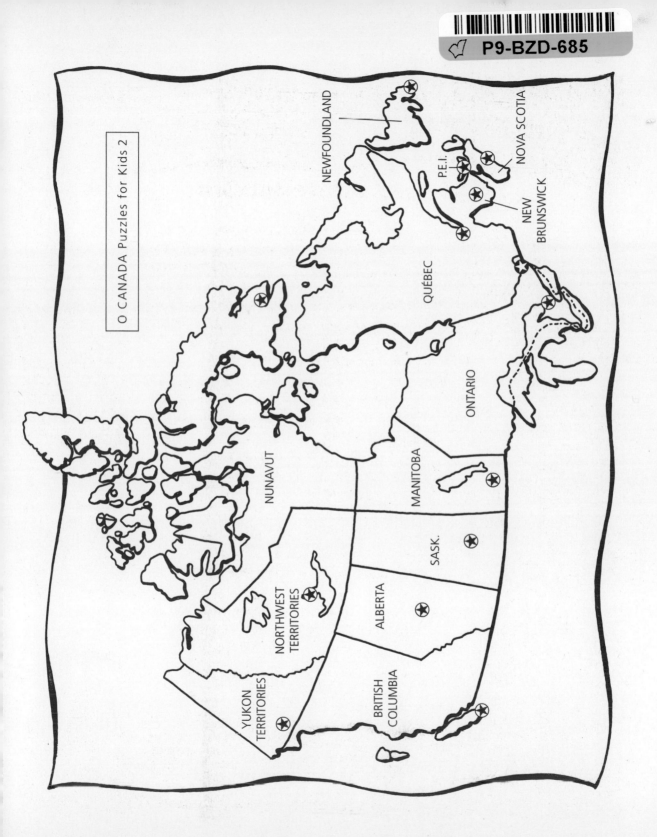

O CANADA Puzzles for Kids 2

O CANADA PUZZLES for KIDS 2

Jesse **Ross** &
Ruth **Porter**

Illustrated by Anne **DeGrace**

BLUEFIELD ⚜ BOOKS

O Canada Puzzles for Kids 2

Published by
Bluefield Books
Gr. 12, C. 9, RR 1, Winlaw, BC   V0G 2J0   1-800-296-6955

Distributed by
Raincoast Books
9050 Shaughnessy Street, Vancouver, BC V6P 6E5   604-323-7100

NATIONAL LIBRARY OF CANADA CATALOGUING IN PUBLICATION DATA
Ross, Jesse, 1986-
  O Canada puzzles for kids / Jesse Ross & Ruth Porter; illustrated by Anne DeGrace.

  ISBN 1-894404-06-8 (bk. 1). — ISBN 1-894404-15-7 (bk. 2)

  1. Puzzles—Juvenile literature. 2. Canada—Miscellanea—Juvenile literature.
I. DeGrace, Anne. II. Porter, Ruth, 1957- III. Title.
FC58 R67 2001   j793.73   C2001-910703-X
F1008.2.R67 2001

Interior illustrations by Anne DeGrace
Cover and interior design by Jim Brennan
Cover folk art by Ric Gerzey (www.freshfolkart.com)

Printed in Canada

5 4 3 2 1

Contents

Contents (continued)

Spot the Difference

Answers

About the Authors

Confused Sports

Unscramble these names of popular sports, but beware — each word contains one extra letter.

1. GAFLO   _____

2. BOOSTFALL   _____

3. TOSSLACER   _____

4. XGINBPO   _____

5. SNECROC   _____

6. LABLABLES   _____

7. YELLVELLBOA   _____

8. BABSLACKLET   _____

9. YOKECUH   _____

10. NITESYN   _____

Unscramble the ten extra letters to reveal the name of a prized trophy.

_____ _____ _____ _____ _____ _____ _____ _____ _____ _____

Lost Letters

Add one letter to each line which will end the left word and start the right word, changing both into Canadian cities or towns. The missing letters, when read from top to bottom, spell the name of a famous Canadian entertainer.

MARKHA	____	AJOR
LUNDA	____	ESOLUTE
FERRYLAN	____	ARTMOUTH
TABE	____	ELIANCE
INVERMER	____	DMUNDSTON
CARCROS	____	YDNEY
KAMLOOP	____	URREY
GATINEA	____	CLUELET
RIVIERE-DU-LOU	____	LENTY

Round and Round

This puzzle goes in a spiral, starting with the top left corner and working around until all the spaces are filled up. The start of the next clue is formed by the last one or two letters of the previous answer. The number in brackets at the end of each clue gives the number of letters in the answer.

CLUES

1. Ocean off our east coast (8)
2. The Titanic hit this (7)
3. Mike Myer's 3rd Austin Power's film (10)
4. Mistake (5)
5. The Toronto Symphony _____ (9)
6. What farmers need in a drought (4)
7. What Eskimoes are now known as (5)
8. Mosquito bites make you _____ (4)
9. Parmesan, gouda or swiss (6)
10. Number of letters in the most populated province (5)
11. Windmills, hydroelectric dams, sunshine all create this (6)
12. Canada's smallest territory (5)
13. Number of provinces that end in a "c" (3)
14. Home for a robin (4)
15. Vancouver's park (7)
16. Are you done? (3)

Your Choice

1. In Alberta it is illegal to call someone a "fat wingless duck" if you are where?

   a) in a hunting lodge;

   b) in the provincial legislature;

   c) in any public building or place.

2. Which Canadian home was originally built with three bowling alleys, a 46-metre shooting gallery, 98 rooms, 25 fireplaces, 5000 electric lights, and a stove big enough to cook an entire steer at one time?

   a) Casa Loma in Toronto;

   b) Jim Carey's Vancouver Island vacation home;

   c) the Prime Minister's official residence.

3. Spike, a 20-year-old elephant who lives at the Calgary Zoo was recently fitted with:

   a) contact lenses;

   b) stainless steel caps for his tusks;

   c) a fibreglass cast for his back right leg.

4. What did Queen Elizabeth II drop that caused such a stir on her 2002 Golden Jubilee Tour?

   a) her purse fell into Victoria harbour where it was picked up by a curious school of dolphins, all of which was recorded by a British film crew;

   b) her pants got accidentally caught on Tom Thompson's canoe and fell down while touring the Museum of Civilization in Ottawa;

   c) the puck at a pre-season Vancouver Canucks hockey game.

5. At midnight on the last day of 1921 the drivers in Victoria, BC all did one thing. What was that?

    a) honked their horns to celebrate the ending of World War I;

    b) were required by law to give up their horse-drawn buggies for automobiles;

    c) changed lanes and began driving on the right-hand side of the road.

6. What is the Canadian Space Agency hoping to send to Mars?

    a) the Canadrill, used for mineral drilling;

    b) a ready-made igloo to test freezing temperatures;

    c) one case of Mars bars (which were originally created in Hamilton, ON).

7. On February 13th, 1999, 1543 couples gathered in Sarnia, ON to set a new world record in:

    a) the largest game of Twister ever held;

    b) most people to ever participate in a three-legged race;

    c) most couples to kiss at the same time in the same place.

Record-Makers

Can you match these world-famous Canadian athletes with their accomplishments?

Clara Hughes _____   Beckie Scott _____

Mike Weir _____   Roland Green _____

Alexandre Despatie _____   Christine Sinclair _____

1. The first Canadian golfer to win the Masters.

2. The first Canadian (and fourth person ever) to win a medal in both the summer and winter Olympic games.

3. This mountain biker won back-to-back world championships in 2001 and 2002.

4. This diver won gold at the 2002 Commonwealth Games, making him the youngest champion in Games' history and putting him in the Guinness Book of World Records.

5. The first North American woman to win an Olympic medal in cross-country skiing.

6. She was named tournament MVP and led Canada to a silver medal at the 2002 FIFA U-19 Women's World Soccer Championship.

Sad, Grouchy and Worthless!

Twenty-one of Canada's saddest place names are hidden in this puzzle; they're written either forwards or backwards, and placed horizontally, vertically or diagonally. At the bottom of the page, fill in the remaining 14 letters in order to find the mystery town.

```
H  G  R  O  U  C  H  Y  A  T
S  U  F  F  E  R  I  N  G  R
N  A  P  E  P  Y  Y  N  A  O
O  N  L  A  M  S  I  D  S  U
I  G  E  R  Y  K  D  S  V  B
S  E  N  T  N  R  E  A  B  L
U  R  M  I  T  L  E  D  O  E
F  S  T  A  H  O  E  S  S  S
N  S  N  T  D  T  R  D  I  O
O  C  R  A  Z  Y  O  T  G  M
C  O  Y  R  R  O  W  N  H  E
W  U  R  Y  M  O  O  L  G  E
```

ANGERS Lake (MB)
Lac de la CONFUSION (QC)
CRAZY Island (NS)
CRY Creek (YT)
DISMAL Lakes (NU)
DOOM Mt. (BC)
FEAR Lake (ON)

GLOOMY Creek (AB)
Lac GROUCHY (QC)
MAD Lake (NWT)
Mt. MISERY (NB)
NOTHING Bay (NL)
ROTTEN Lake (MB)
SAD Lake (ON)

SIGH Lake (ON)
SOB Lake (SK)
STINKING Gulch (NB)
SUFFERING Pond (NS)
TROUBLESOME Cove (NL)
WORRY Lake (AB)
WORTHLESS Creek (BC)

_ _ _ _ _   _ _ _ _ _ _ _ _ _ (NL)

(**Note**: For this puzzle, only the words in capitals are included, i.e. for GLOOMY Creek, only GLOOMY is hidden. The provincial abbreviations are included here for information only.)

Dream Teams

We've mixed a couple of phony names into the following list of sports teams —
can you guess which two they are?

Calgary Storm

Dawson City Sumos

Sainte-Julie Panthers

Erie Otters

Ottawa Renegades

Montreal Express

Iqaluit Iceslingers

Halifax Mooseheads

_____   _____

Juggling Jugglers

Two of our jugglers are identical, while the remaining ones are all a bit different.
Which two are the same?

1 2 3 4 5 6

_____   _____

Puzzling Letters

In this puzzle you're trying to figure out the three words listed at the bottom — one of the most thrillings shows you'll ever see. We've given you four clues. Fill in as many as you can, then transfer the letters from the clues to the numbers at the bottom.

a) ___ ___ ___ ___ ___   An old-fashioned pen
   4   8 13 11 14

b) ___ ___ ___ ___   The centre of something
   1 10   3   6

c) ___ ___ ___ ___   Necessary equipment for the Yukon Quest
   9 14 12   7

d) ___ ___ ___   What you give to someone when you borrow
   2 10   5   money

Answer

___ ___ ___ ___ ___ ___ ___ ___ ___ ___ ___ ___ ___ ___
 1   2   3   4   5   6   7   8   9 10 11 12 13 14

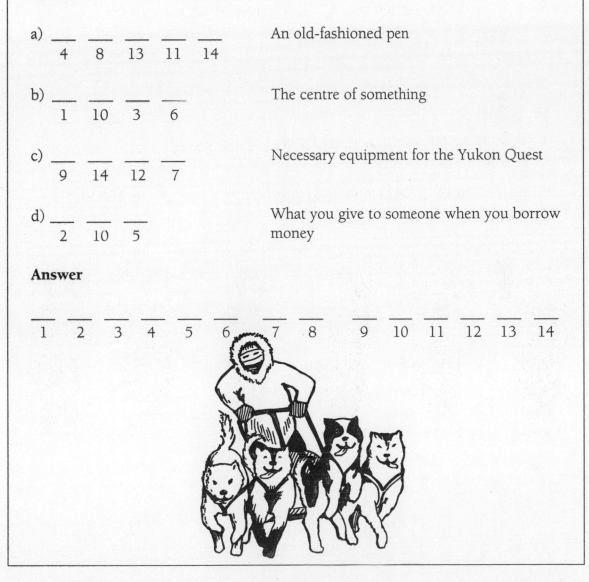

Swim, Run and Fly

Fit the names of various animals, birds and fish into their proper places in the puzzle squares. Each word is used only once. We've started you off by filling in COD. Can you spot the one made-up name?

3 letters
~~COD~~

4 letters
CROW

GOAT

LOON

SWAN

SEAL

SORA

5 letters
BEARS

EIDER

OTTER

SHEEP

SNAKE

WHALE

6 letters
BELUGA

BOBCAT

SCOTER

SHRIMP

7 letters
PELICAN

SEA LION

TADPOLE

VULTURE

8 letters
BOBWHITE

CARDINAL

ICEFLIER

OLDSQUAW

PHEASANT

SHOVELER

RACCOONS

9 letters
ALBATROSS

BALD EAGLE

WOLVERINE

WOODCHUCK

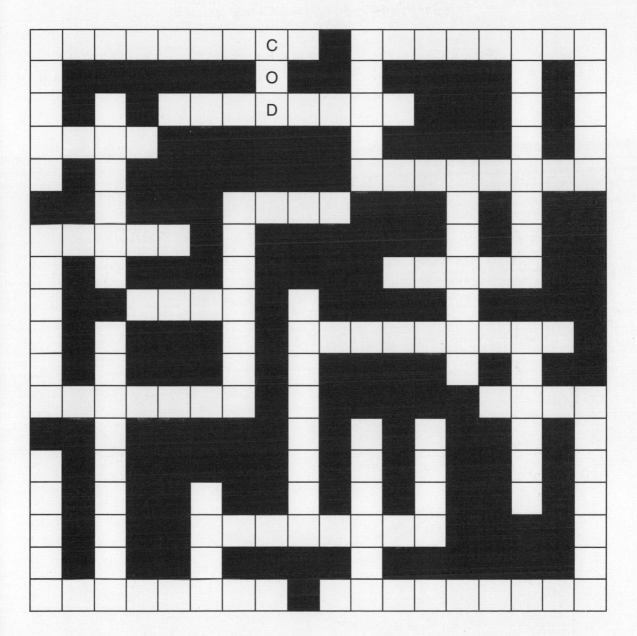

Spot the Difference: Skate Park

There are at least 16 differences between these two pages; how many can you spot?

Wild Canada

We've hidden the names of six flowers in this puzzle. You won't find all of them in the wild, but they are in many Canadian gardens. They all start from the middle letter P and can be found in any direction, though rarely in a straight line.

Here are three to get you started: Petunia, Phlox, Peony.

R	Y	S	A	I
M	R	O	N	N
I	A	A	S	U
Y	R	**P**	E	T
P	E	O	H	O
I	P	N	L	A
P	X	O	Y	X

Famous Canadians

The goal here is to match the people in the left-hand column with their "claim to fame" listed in the right column.

Craig Keilburger	Star junior hockey player from Rankin Inlet
Cindy Klassen	TV sports host and amateur referee
Jennifer Robinson	Musician, writer and TV host
Jordin Tootoo	Anthropologist, world-renowed orangutan expert
Jann Arden	Youth activist, Free the Children founder
Joel Wapnick	Writer of O Canada in 1880
Ron MacLean	World Scrabble Champion 1999
Jian Ghomeshi	Author of *Everest* and *Macdonald Hall* series
Calixa Lavallee	Six-time Canadian Figure Skating Champion
Gordon Korman	Pop singer and student of classical piano
Chantal Kreviazuk	2003 World Champion, long track speed skating
Moses Znaimer	TV creator of Muchmusic and other shows
Birute Galdikas	Singer song-writer and former video-store clerk

The Cars

Coach asks you to put the bag of balls into his car. But now you're in the parking lot you've forgotten which car is his. See if you can figure it out from these clues.

#1   #2   #3

a) coach has four kids but only one car;

b) he's never been north of Lake Superior;

c) besides soccer he loves any sport that gets you moving fast;

d) coach's youngest child is the goalkeeper for your team.

e) the numbers on his license plate add up to an even number.

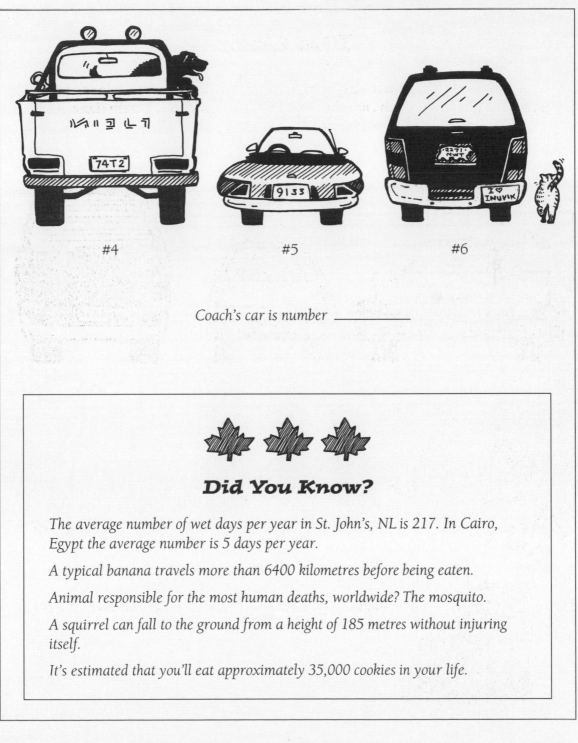

#4

#5

#6

Coach's car is number _____

Did You Know?

The average number of wet days per year in St. John's, NL is 217. In Cairo, Egypt the average number is 5 days per year.

A typical banana travels more than 6400 kilometres before being eaten.

Animal responsible for the most human deaths, worldwide? The mosquito.

A squirrel can fall to the ground from a height of 185 metres without injuring itself.

It's estimated that you'll eat approximately 35,000 cookies in your life.

Weather Wonders

Rumours are swirling that in a recent poll (we're not sure if it was a north pole or a south pole), more than 73% of Canadians said that their favourite topic of conversation was the weather. Whether this can be scientifically proven is unsure, but there is one thing we can predict — the weather will be a hot topic of conversation in some part of Canada today.

1. What is an ice road?
   a) the name given to rivers that are used as roads during the Arctic winter;
   b) the nickname for the NHL's playoff race to the Stanley Cup;
   c) the route taken by the dogsled racers in the Yukon Quest.

2. What is February 6th's claim to fame?
   a) it is the shortest day of the year;
   b) it is Groundhog Day;
   c) on average it is the coldest day of the year.

3. In a 1923 tornado a Saskatchewan man lost something and later found it in a tree one kilometre from his home. What did he lose?
   a) a calf; b) his pants; c) his tractor.

4. Prince Rupert, BC ranks in the Top 10 of the cloudiest places on earth.

True or *False*

5. Which of these is the driest place in Canada?
   a) Arctic Bay, NU;
   b) Osoyoos, BC;
   c) Frontier, SK

6. When a chunk breaks off of an iceberg, it is known as hatching.

True or *False*

7. On very cold days what's the most important thing you can do to protect your pets when they are outside?
   a) keep them from running around too much so they don't overheat;
   b) smear Vaseline on the pads of their feet;
   c) silly as it sounds, a head covering protects animals just like it does humans.

8. Just after Christmas each year thousands of Canadians take part in an annual count — what are they counting?
   a) outdoor ice rinks;
   b) the icicles on West Edmonton Mall;
   c) birds.

Boggling Letters

The letters below spell out Yellowknife. How many words of four letters or more can you make by mixing up these 11 letters?

Good Sports

1. Which professional athlete is nicknamed *Team Canada*?
    a) Steve Nash;
    b) Vince Carter;
    c) Mike Weir;
    d) Melanie Turgeon.

2. Hugo Girard is a multiple winner of both the Canadian and North American Strongest Man competitions. How many times did he once lift a medium-sized car?
    a) 3 times;
    b) 10 times;
    c) 15 times;
    d) 17 times.

3. Which of the following events has *never* been a part of the World's Strongest Man competition?
    a) flipping a 400 kilogram tire 30 metres;
    b) pulling a Boeing 737 plane using only a harness and rope;
    c) carrying five grown men 30 metres, all at the same time;
    d) using a harness and rope, pulling a 17,275 kg. truck 30 metres.

4. In 1982 Brock Alison crossed Canada from Vancouver to Halifax in 56 days. How did he do it?
    a) on a unicycle;
    b) on snowshoes;
    c) in a glider;
    d) by wheelchair.

5. On February 24th, 2002 more than 10.5 million Canadians were doing the same thing. What was that?
   - a) filing their income tax;
   - b) setting a new Guiness Book of World Records for most people playing one sport (basketball) at a single time;
   - c) watching the Quebec Winter Carnival parade;
   - d) watching on TV as the Canadian men's hockey team played for gold at the Salt Lake City Olympics.

6. Every August the town of Macklin, SK hosts the World Championship Bunnock Tournament, with a total prize of $20,000. What is Bunnock?
   - a) the official name for Table Hockey;
   - b) it involves throwing horse ankle bones at other horse ankle bones, with the purpose of knocking over your opponent's bones;
   - c) running cross-country track while carrying another person on your back;
   - d) a cross between polo and soccer, played underwater.

7. On August 3rd, 2001 a baseball game between the Toronto Blue Jays and Baltimore Orioles had to be stopped mid-game. Why?
   - a) swarms of aphids descended on the stadium;
   - b) a freak hailstorm struck before the SkyDome roof could be closed;
   - c) a flock of Canada geese landed in centre field and wouldn't be chased off;
   - d) fog rolled in off Lake Superior resulting in a whiteout.

8. Toronto's Pete Lovering is the 2002 World Champion — in what sport?
   - a) Scrabble;
   - b) Bunnock;
   - c) Rock Paper Scissors;
   - d) Ultimate Frisbee.

Eureka!

Sixteen Canadian inventions are hidden in this puzzle; they're written either forwards or backwards, and placed horizontally, vertically or diagonally. At the bottom of the page, fill in the remaining 14 letters, in order, to reveal this very striking invention.

```
S   F   B   R   E   P   P   I   Z   G
G   N   A   F   N   E   U   Q   O   T
N   A   S   I   O   V   A   A   E   H
I   M   K   P   H   G   L   V   S   I
D   R   E   N   P   I   H   A   A   P
N   E   T   B   E   O   D   O   I   J
I   P   B   M   L   R   W   H   R   L
B   U   A   Y   E   K   C   O   H   N
I   S   L   D   T   V   V   T   A   I
K   N   L   A   C   R   O   S   S   E
S   A   M   R   A   D   A   N   A   C
B   L   U   B   T   H   G   I   L   G
```

ATV	HOCKEY	SUPERMAN
BALDERDASH	JAVA (computer language)	TELEPHONE
BASKETBALL	LACROSSE	TOQUE
CANADARM	LIGHTBULB	VCHIP
FOGHORN	SKI BINDINGS	ZIPPER
GOALIE MASK		

— — — — — — — — — — — — — —

Canadiana

ACROSS

  1 Alberta city where the dinosaurs once roamed, now home to the Tyrell Museum
  7 When you flip a coin, it's the opposite of tails
  9 A tasty baked dessert often made from apples and topped with ice cream
 10 Where peas and whales gather
 12 What's ____?
 14 This product first linked Canada and has traditionally been made in Hamilton.
 16 If your "barn door" is open, what should you do up?
 17 This type of bear draws tourists to Churchill, Manitoba each winter
 20 The large region of northern Canada that has permafrost and lacks tall trees
 23 Marc Garneau, Roberta Bondar and Chris Hadfield
 25 The item that replaced the one dollar bill
 26 Bran, blueberry or banana nut

DOWN

  1 Mallards and eiders and the hockey team Paul Kariya plays on
  2 _____ Nations, a world organization based in New York
  3 The opposite of sad
  4 What sailors lost at sea like to see
  5 An expression many Canadians use at the end of their questions
  6 This mid-Alberta city is halfway between the Flames and the Oilers
  8 The abbreviation for the middle Prairie province
 11 The French-speaking city across the river from Ottawa
 13 The earth's atmosphere
 14 A long thin piece of land, or stuff that comes out of your mouth
 15 Orangutan, gibbon, gorilla or chimpanzee
 16 The brand name for the machine that cleans the ice at most hockey games
 18 Even and ____
 19 The largest Canadian island
 21 You need one of these to play soccer, golf, and squash
 22 What salmon or tuna are often packaged in
 24 The number of official languages in Canada

Dumb Laws

Check out these wacky Canadian laws. All are still valid, but most aren't actually enforced. Beware, we've put in two made-up laws — can you figure out which two?

1. It is illegal to remove bandages in public in Canada.

2. In Nova Scotia it's illegal for a person to water their lawn when it's raining.

3. It is illegal to kill a sasquatch in British Columbia.

4. In Nunavut it is illegal to wear shorts in a public place from November 15th to March 31st.

5. In Fort Qu'Appelle, Saskatchewan all teenagers walking down the main street must have their shoe laces tied, or else face a fine.

6. Street musicians in Victoria, BC aren't allowed to give balloon animals to children.

7. It's illegal to play video games for more than two hours a day or watch more than three hours of TV a day in Prince Edward Island.

8. You are not allowed to spit on the street in Montreal.

9. It's illegal to bring a slingshot into any National Park, even if you don't use it.

10. You can be put in jail for up to two years if you are caught offending a public place with a bad smell, anywhere in Canada.

The two fake laws are _____ and _____.

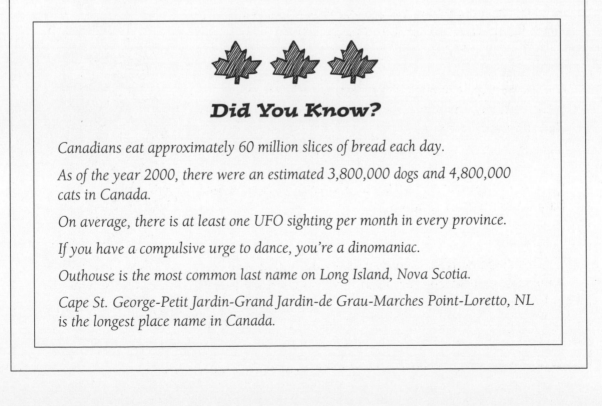

Did You Know?

Canadians eat approximately 60 million slices of bread each day.

As of the year 2000, there were an estimated 3,800,000 dogs and 4,800,000 cats in Canada.

On average, there is at least one UFO sighting per month in every province.

If you have a compulsive urge to dance, you're a dinomaniac.

Outhouse is the most common last name on Long Island, Nova Scotia.

Cape St. George-Petit Jardin-Grand Jardin-de Grau-Marches Point-Loretto, NL is the longest place name in Canada.

Musical Mix-Up

Match the band or artist in the left-hand column with their song on the right.

Rascal2   Complicated

The Tragically Hip   Heaven Only Knows

Sarah Harmer   Hands Clean

K-OS   On The Radio

David Usher   Somewhere Out There

Barenaked Ladies   Still Waiting

Nelly Furtado   Pinch Me

Sum 41   Don't Get Your Back Up

Our Lady Peace   How You Remind Me

Nickleback   My Way Out

Avril Lavigne   Crazy World

Alanis Morissette   It's A Good Life If You Don't Weaken

Money Problems

1. Have you ever wondered what happens to all those coins people toss into public fountains? Are they:
> a) returned to the Bank of Canada and then reissued;
> b) donated to charities;
> c) left for whoever needs the extra cash.

2. You have five coins in your pocket — added together they are worth 55 cents. What coins are they?

3. If you have only half of a $20 bill is it worth anything?
> a) it's worth the full value as long as you can still see what dollar value the bill is;
> b) you are out of luck; the bill can only be missing 1/4 of its original size to be worth anything;
> c) half of a $20 bill is worth $10.

4. In Canada's early history, coins were often in short supply. The government once gave French soldiers these to use in place of coins:
> a) specially-marked playing cards;
> b) drilled shells;
> c) wooden nickels.

5. The 1911 silver dollar is said to be Canada's rarest coin — there are only two or three in existence today. In January 2003, one of these was sold at a coin auction in New York for:
> a) $50,000;
> b) $500,000;
> c) $1,000,000.

Campbellford, ON is home to Canada's largest toonie, built in honour of local resident Brent Townsend who created the polar bear image on the original coin. The coin is over 8 metres high and 5.5 metres wide.

If you're interested in coins visit the website of The Royal Canadian Mint (www.mint.ca).

What's My Sport?

Try to guess the answer in as few questions as possible.

#1 _____

a) I'm played on a big field with two goals.

b) The players are always holding something in their hands.

c) Both teams are fighting over a small, hard ball.

d) It's Canada's national summer sport.

#2 _____

a) Two opponents are in a small enclosed room.

b) You can use the walls for greater success.

c) Try and stay out of the way of your opponent's racket!

d) One of the top players in the world is Canada's Jonathan Power.

#3 _____

a) You're going up, and down, and then up again, and then down again.

b) For the highest score you need to add lots of flips and spins.

c) Your equipment begins with a metal frame, some springs and ....

d) You'll find the basic equipment in lots of backyards, but it takes years of training before you'll be able to do a Dolphin or a Randolph.

Highland Dancers

Two of our dancers are identical, while the remaining ones are all a bit different. Which two are the same?

1   2   3   4   5   6

_____   _____

Giant Statues

What is it with Canadians and large statues? You can spot them everywhere — from the Viking in Gimli, Manitoba to Colborne, Ontario's giant apple to the world famous lobster in Shediac, New Brunswick — hundreds all over the country. In Saskatchewan alone we counted 79 different giant statues!

Can you match the statue below with the town it can be found in? (If you can get five or more correct, maybe one day you'll have your own giant statue erected in your honour!)

Tin Soldier	Glenboro, MB
Lumberjack	Stewiacke, NS
Hockey Cards	Goobies, NL
Fiddle	Vegreville, AB
Camel	Montreal, QC
Milk Bottle	Kelvington, SK
Mastodon	Upsala, ON
Easter Egg (Pysanka)	Kedgwick, NB
Mosquito carrying a man	New Westminster, BC
Moose	Cavendish, PE

For more (lots more) giant Canadian statues visit The Big Things of a Big Country website (www.bigthings.ca).

Lost Letters #2

Add one letter to each line which will end the left word and start the right word, changing both into Canadian cities or towns. The missing letters, when read from top to bottom, spell the name of an early inhabitant of North America.

BATTLEFOR ＿＿ EVON ISLAND

PORT ALBERN ＿＿ NUVIK

HAMILTO ＿＿ UTAK

RICHIBUCT ＿＿ UTREMONT

SOURI ＿＿ NOWFLAKE

VICTORI ＿＿ LTONA

PICTO ＿＿ PSALA

VANIE ＿＿ OSSLAND

Common Ground

1. What do Jonathan Cheechoo, Craig Berube and Gino Odjick have in common?
 a) they are all NHL hockey players of native descent;
 b) they are members of the band Stoney Park;
 c) they biked across Canada in the nude, protesting the high prices of blue jeans.

2. What do golf, tug-of-war and waterskiing have in common?
 a) all were once official Olympic sports;
 b) they are listed as Prime Minister Jean Chretien's three favourite sports;
 c) they have been officially declared as "dangerous" to Canadians in a 2002 study conducted at the University of Waterloo.

3. What do Moscow, Copenhagen and Dublin have in common?
 a) in each of these cities there is an area nicknamed "Little Canada";
 b) they are all towns in Ontario;
 c) they have all, at one time, been sister cities to Moncton, NB.

4. What do the Maple Leaf flag, Shania Twain and Mario Lemieux have in common?
 a) they were all introduced or born in 1965;
 b) absolutely nothing;
 c) they were prominently featured in the 2003 Academy Awards.

5. What do Haircut Lake, Headless Creek and Mount Braine have in common?
 a) they are all fake place names;
 b) gold found at each of these sites triggered gold rushes;
 c) they are all places found in Yukon.

6. What do Mathieu Turcotte, Jonathan Guilmette and Francois-Louis Tremblay have in common?

     a) they are members of Canada's award-winning ice sculpture team;

     b) they make up the Cirque du Soleil's world famous high-wire acrobatic team;

     c) along with short track speed skater Marc Gagnon they won gold at the 2002 Olympic Winter Games in the 5000 metre relay.

7. What do a Jolly Jumper, a paint roller and a foghorn have in common?

     a) they were three props used during Avril Lavigne's 2002 concert tour;

     b) they were all invented by Canadians;

     c) they are the only three products Canada exports to France.

8. What do Efisga, Tuponia and Colonia have in common?

     a) they are all communities in Nunavut;

     b) they were all proposed names for what is now, (thank goodness!) Canada;

     c) they were different names for slab ice as recorded by John Franklin during his search for the Northwest Passage.

9. What do the Finger Pull, Knuckle Hop and Two-foot-high Kick have in common?

     a) they used to be mandatory warm-up exercises in the Grade 7 Phys Ed. curriculum;

     b) they are the titles of Dr. Seuss' first three published children's books;

     c) they are all events in the Dene/Inuit Games segment of the Arctic Winter Games.

What Am I?

Can you figure out what these clues point to? Try to get the answer in as few clues as possible.

#1 _____

a) I was an extremely popular event during the 1800s.

b) I began around 1858 in northern BC and Yukon.

c) You could say I was like the modern day lottery.

d) I've left behind a trail of ghost towns.

#2 _____

a) I've brought Canada over $900 million in sales even though only five of me have ever been sold.

b) I was first operated on November 3, 1981, thousands of kilometres above the earth.

c) I've been a great help to NASA.

d) So far I've been on 63 successful missions, including helping to repair the Hubble Space Telescope.

#3 _____

a) I am more than 800 kilometres across at my greatest width.

b) I'm covered in pack ice for at least four months every year.

c) I am a huge inland sea, joined to the Arctic Ocean to the north.

d) I share the same name as Canada's oldest company.

Did You Know?

The game of lacrosse is estimated to be 600 years old.

St. Paul, Alberta is home to the world's first flying saucer (UFO) landing pad.

A good healthy sneeze has the same velocity as a hurricane.

Moose were once used to haul mail in the Edmonton area.

According to Guiness, 75-year-old BC resident Wong Yui Hoi is the world's oldest snowboarder.

There's a golf course near Stratford, Ontario that uses llamas as caddies.

Puzzling Letters #2

The object of this puzzle is to figure out the two words listed at the bottom — a truly amazing sight. We've given you four clues. Fill in as many as you can, then transfer the letters from the clues to the numbers at the bottom.

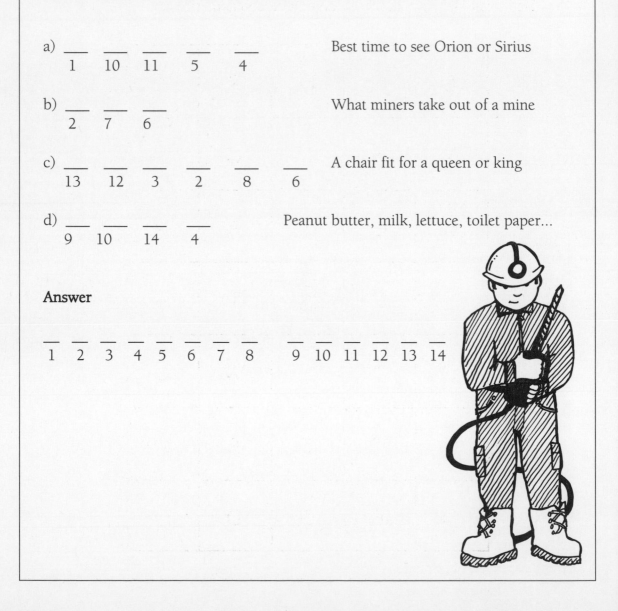

a) ___ ___ ___ ___ ___   Best time to see Orion or Sirius
    1   10   11   5   4

b) ___ ___ ___   What miners take out of a mine
    2   7   6

c) ___ ___ ___ ___ ___ ___   A chair fit for a queen or king
   13   12   3   2   8   6

d) ___ ___ ___ ___   Peanut butter, milk, lettuce, toilet paper...
    9   10   14   4

Answer

___ ___ ___ ___ ___ ___ ___ ___   ___ ___ ___ ___ ___ ___
  1   2   3   4   5   6   7   8   9   10   11   12   13   14

Wild Canada #2

We've hidden the names of six fish in this puzzle. They all start from the middle letter S and can be found in any direction, but rarely in a straight line.

Here are three to get you started: Sculpin, Sturgeon and Stingray.

E	O	M	R	A
L	N	L	G	Y
H	O	I	A	N
S	P	**S**	T	I
L	I	C	W	U
N	U	F	R	O
O	E	G	D	G

Famous First Words

Here are the first lines of nine well-known books — can you match them to the title and author listed below?

1. Being a weather forecaster in Canada is not easy.

2. "I'm gonna hurl!"

3. A mother held her new baby and very slowly rocked him back and forth, back and forth, back and forth.

4. There were five children, counting the Pollywog, and their names all began with the letter P.

5. Wings trimmed tight, Shade sailed through the forest.

6. "Our whole family is going on a trip across Canada."

7. Our boat was the greatest — a classic cruiser called the *Amor de Cosmos*.

8. The winters of my childhood were long, long seasons.

9. Jelly Belly bit / With a big fat bite.

Wow Canada, *Vivien Bowers* _____

The Hockey Sweater, *Roch Carrier* _____

The Screech Owls' Northern Adventure, *Roy MacGregor* _____

Love You Forever, *Robert Munsch* _____

Jelly Belly, *Dennis Lee* _____

Sunwing, *Kenneth Oppel* _____

Emily Carr Mystery, *Eric Wilson* _____

The Secret World of Og, *Pierre Berton* _____

The Day Niagara Falls Ran Dry, *David Phillips* _____

Rainbow Country

Each of the words listed below are part of a word or phrase that answers the questions below. They are people, places or things. Each word is only used once and every answer starts with a colour.

GREEN	BLACK	BLUE	HORSE	RED	GARBAGE
CREEK	GREEN	VILLE	BAGS	PINK	NOSE
PEACE	BLUE	RIVER	ORANGE	RED	RODEO
WHITE	GREEN	FLAMINGOS			

1. ___ _____   A funny man, with his own TV show

2. _____   Ontario town

3. ___ _____   Site of an enormous flood in 1997

4. _____ _____ ____   Invented by a Canadian

5. ____ _____   Well-known band

6. _____   Found on the Canadian dime

7. _____   Capital city of Yukon

8. _____ _____   Pioneer Village outside of Toronto

9. ____ _____   Used to scare away osprey in AB, and as a lawn decoration

10. _____   Organization of activists originally from Vancouver

Spot the Difference: Winter

There are at least 16 differences between these two pages; how many can you spot?

Action Canada

Fit the names of various sports and activities into their proper places in the puzzle squares on the next page. Each word is used only once. We've started you off by filling in TIE.

3 letters
ACT
EAT
MOW
RAP
SIT
SKI
~~TIE~~

4 letters
COOK
CURL
DIVE
DRAW
HIKE
JUMP
MUSH
PASS
PUTT
SING
SKIP
SLAM
SLED
SWIM
TREK
YOGA

5 letters
CHECK
DANCE
DREAM
KAYAK
PEDAL
SKATE
SLIDE
SWING
VAULT
WRITE

6 letters
DEFEND
GIGGLE
PADDLE
SLALOM
SWEEPS
TACKLE

8 letters
TELEMARK

7 letters
COMPETE
EDUCATE
SKIJUMP
WRIGGLE

Body Parts

We've hidden 24 unusual place names in this word search; they're written either forwards or backwards, and placed horizontally, vertically or diagonally. At the bottom of the page, fill in the remaining 14 letters in order to get down to the bare bones.

```
S  H  K  T  O  O  F  A  E  N
L  D  E  R  L  E  R  N  Y  I
L  K  A  A  E  M  N  O  S  E
U  I  T  E  R  G  O  G  P  V
K  D  B  H  H  T  N  G  I  D
S  N  O  D  N  E  S  I  L  O
N  E  N  A  I  L  L  N  F  O
E  Y  E  B  R  O  W  B  C  L
K  E  V  U  A  L  A  H  O  B
O  O  L  T  E  C  E  J  A  W
R  T  Y  T  K  S  K  C  E  N
B  M  U  H  T  T  O  O  T  H
```

BACK Brook (NB)
BAD HEART (AB)
BLOODVEIN River (MB)
BONE Brook (NB)
BROKEN SKULL River (NT)
BUTT Lake (ON)
CHEST Island (BC)
ELBOW (SK)
EYEBROW (SK)

FINGER Mountain (YT)
FOOT Cape (NS)
HEART'S Delight (NL)
KIDNEY Bay (NU)
King's HEAD (NS)
Lac NECK (QC)
Lac NOSE (QC)
Lac TOE (QC)

LIPSY Lake (ON)
Moose JAW (SK)
NAIL Pond (PE)
NOGGIN Cove (NL)
Salmon ARM (BC)
THUMB Island (NT)
TOOTH Ridge (NU)

_ _ _ _ _ _ _ _ _ _ _ _ _ _ (NU)

(**Note**: For this puzzle, only the words in capitals are included, i.e. for Moose JAW, only JAW is hidden. Once again, provincial abbreviations are included here for information only.)

More Choices

1. Altona, Manitoba is:
   a) the gopher capital of Canada;
   b) the only Canadian city situated directly on the 49th parallel;
   c) the geographic centre of North America.

2. 16 metres is:
   a) the height of the highest point of land in Saskatchewan;
   b) the height of high tide in the Bay of Fundy;
   c) the length of an average adult orca or killer whale.

3. Each fall there is a large gathering near the town of Churchill, MB. Who are they and what are they there for?
   a) polar bears waiting for the ice on Hudson Bay to thicken enough to bear their weight;
   b) annual convention of geophysicists who measure the depth of the ice on Hudson Bay;
   c) the Winston Churchill fan club, who meet here to test the dedication of each member.

4. New Brunswick's Skedaddle Ridge is named for:
   a) American draft dodgers who escaped over this ridge into Canada during the Civil War;
   b) extreme winter sports athletes who gather here each year to snowboard and ski;
   c) Ichabod Skedaddle, the first premier of New Brunswick.

5. BC farmer Nick Parsons protested cuts to rural farms by driving from his home near Dawson Creek to Parliament Hill in Ottawa. What was he driving?
   a) a 1912 Ford pick-up truck named RIP, short for Rest In Peace;
   b) a combine named Prairie Belle;
   c) a team of horses, nicknamed Rural Initiatives.

6. In 1976 a new island was discovered in Canada's north by using satellite imagery. The island is now named:
   a) Uk'saut Island;
   b) Island 483360-1a;
   c) Landsat Island.

7. On the TV show Saturday Night Live, Avril Lavigne wore one of her old soccer shirts, which created a huge demand from her fans. It featured the logo of a local business. Was it:
   a) Paul's Plumbing;
   b) Home Hardware;
   c) Antonio's Pizza and Ribs.

8. Men With Brooms, one of Canada's most popular movies, had many scenes filmed in:
   a) a curling rink;
   b) an office building;
   c) an elementary school.

9. One of the traditional sports in the Arctic Winter Games is the Snowsnake. Is the object of the game:
   a) to see how far you can throw a frozen snake;
   b) to see how many people you can get to lie down on the snow in the form of a snake;
   c) to see how far you can throw a spear underhand on the snow.

Where Am I?

See if you can locate which province or territory we're talking about, by the clues given below.

1. I'm home to Canada's largest collection of totem poles, longest free ferry ride, and rainiest cities. _____

2. Many European immigrants first landed in my largest city, which was the scene of the largest peacetime explosion in Canadian history. I'm also home to many of Canada's pioneering black families. _____

3. I'm home to a well-known folk festival in Birds Hill Park, the windiest street in the country, and the grave of Louis Riel. _____

4. I'm the most crowded province, but there's still room for Anne and Stompin' Tom. _____

5. I was the original home of the Beothuks, am a great place to view icebergs and whales, and I'm divided into two parts. _____

6. I'm home to many elevators that don't go up or down, whooping cranes, and some pretty famous curlers. _____

7. I've got rich aboriginal traditions and am a place where nature rules. I recently lost a lot of ground, but I'm still home to Canada's largest national park.

_____

Across Canada

ACROSS

1 Mike Weir and Lori Kane's favourite sport
3 Christine Sinclair and Owen Hargreaves's favourite sport
6 The tree that acorns come from
8 Royal Hudson, GO, VIA, E&N, etc.
9 This type of corn was a major food crop for native people
10 One of the traditional Canadian industries
15 Another name for couch or chesterfield
16 The largest city in Atlantic Canada
18 Don't panic, it's just a certain type of clock
19 Louis Riel was an early leader of these people
22 The largest member of the deer family
23 The 17th letter of the English alphabet
24 This "killer" is found in all three of our oceans

DOWN

2 What's red on our flag and blue on a Toronto hockey sweater
3 JK Rowling read to more than 20,000 people in this building
4 A popular activity in Banff, Algonquin, Gros Morne and other parks
5 This great lake isn't as scary as it sounds
6 The name of this province, which is almost 1/5th water, came from a native word meaning "beautiful water"
7 This fish-eating mammal lives in the waters off all three coasts
8 Ontario hometown and location of the Shania Twayne Centre
11 Nine, in French
12 This type of hunt was the basis for the Plains Indians way of life
13 Bay that's at the southern end of Hudson Bay
14 What loggers never used to be without
17 Friend, in French
18 Quarterbacks and pitchers both need a good one of these
20 The Newfoundland-based band Great Big _____
21 The postal code abbreviation for the smallest province

Who Am I?

Can you figure out who these clues point to? Try to get the answer in as few clues as possible.

#1 _____

a) I've won medals in the last three Olympic Winter Games, at Lillehjammer, Nagano and Salt Lake City.

b) I like anything that goes fast.

c) In the 2002 Olympics I won three medals in short track speed skating: gold in the men's 1500m, bronze in the 500m and another gold in the men's 5000m relay.

d) My last name sounds a lot like the word "win" in French.

#2 _____

a) I sang gospel in church choirs and taught myself guitar when I was 12.

b) My name is French for a spring month.

c) When asked about my work, I once said, "It's a pretty nice job, and better than sitting in an office typing all day."

d) I won four Juno awards in 2003 for Best Single, Album, New Artist and Pop Album of the Year.

#3 _____

a) I had my own TV show from 1967 until 1996.

b) My first name is Ernie but most everyone calls me Mr.

c) I was never one to brag but I did win a special Save the Children Award and I'm a member of the Order of Canada.

d) Do Casey and Finnegan ring any bells?

Did You Know?

Alexander Graham Bell may have invented the telephone, but he refused to have one in his study — the ringing drove him nuts.

It's impossible to lick your elbow.

The English language has nearly one million different words, while French has less than 100,000 words.

The five most frequently used letters of the alphabet are E, T, O, A and N — the least used are K, J, X, Z and Q.

OK is the most used expression of any language on earth.

Soccer is the most popular sport in the world.

Confused Rivers

The following sets of letters are mixed-up Canadian rivers. See if you can unravel them — but beware, each has one extra letter.

1. R S E F V R A _____

2. H L O H C R L I U C _____

3. V E Y R S N E _____

4. D A R E _____

5. C G P E E A _____

6. G Y E A E A S N U _____

7. M K U Z I E N E A C _____

8. C O L R B U M I A _____

Unravel the eight extra letters to discover an early Canadian river traveller.

— — — — — — — —

Note:
This is a tricky puzzle, so we've given you 20 rivers to choose your eight scambled ones from.

Churchill, Columbia, Don, Fraser, Mackenzie, Moose, Nass, Natashquan, Ottawa, Peace, Porcupine, Red, Rupert, Saguenay, Saint John, Saskatchewan, Severn, Skeena, St. Lawrence, Yukon .

Odd One Out

In each group below, there is one word, name or phrase that doesn't belong. Can you find the one that doesn't fit?

VJs
Namugenyi (Nam) Kiwanuka   Rick Campanelli
George Stroumboulopoulos   Red 1

CANADIAN WORLD RECORDS
world's longest coastline
world's oldest snowboarder
world's heaviest single-day snowfall
world's largest cherry pie

POLITICIANS
Sheila Copps   Robert Munsch   Jean Chretien   Sir John A. Macdonald

COMEDIANS
Luba Goy   Lorne Elliott   Adrienne Clarkson   Tom Green

BANDS
DL Incognito   Missing Link   Nickelback   Painting Daisies

ACTORS
Anna Paquin   Justin Trudeau   Mike Myers   Neve Campbell

NEWFOUNDLAND PLACE NAMES
Puddle Pond   Fogarty's Cove   Fall off the Island   Nickey's Nose Cove

ATHLETES
Hazel Mae   Hayley Wickenheiser   Erin McLeod   Cindy Klassen

You're A What?

1. If you live in Moose Jaw, are you a:
   a) Moose Javian;
   b) Moose Jawbonian;
   c) Mooseaminnian.

2. If you live in Newfoundland, are you a:
   a) Newfoundlandite;
   b) Newfoundlandian;
   c) Newfoundlander.

3. If you live in Yellowknife, are you a:
   a) Yellowknifer;
   b) Yellowknovian;
   c) Yellowknives.

4. If you live in Halifax, are you a:
   a) Haligonian;
   b) Halifaxian;
   c) Haliwegian.

5. If you live in Saskatoon, are you a:
   a) Saskwatch;
   b) Saskatoonie;
   c) Saskatonian.

6. If you live in Labrador, are you a:
   a) Labradorite;
   b) Labradorian;
   c) Labragonian.

7. If you live in Victoria, are you a:
   a) Victorarian;
   b) Victorious;
   c) Victorian.

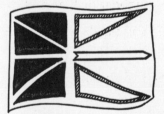

Round and Round Again

This puzzle goes in a spiral, starting with the top left corner and working around until all the spaces are filled. The start of the next clue is formed by the last one or two letters of the previous answer. The number in brackets at the end of each clue gives the number of letters in the answer.

CLUES

1. This gold rush attracted more than 100,000 prospectors (8)

2. This seaweed is a rich natural source of iron (4)

3. Person who drives a tugboat or flies a plane (5)

4. You need a ticket to win one of these (7)

5. The colour of snow you don't want to eat (6)

6. A young owl (5)

7. a d q u p l x etc. (7)

8. Rain mixed with snow or hail (5)

9. Keeps your head warm in winter (5)

10. A direction (4)

11. What every letter needs (5)

12. In one of these you might see clowns, floats and marching bands (6)

13. Not alive (4)

14. To find something new (8)

15. Some say you'll find a pot of gold at the end of one of these (7)

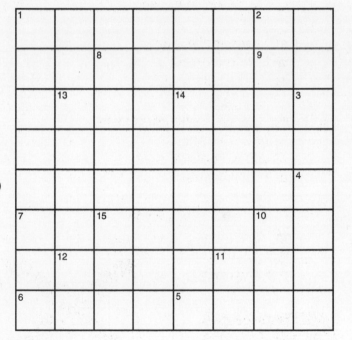

ANSWERS

Please note: To the best of our knowledge, all answers were accurate as of July 2003.

Confused Sports (page 7)
1. Golf
2. Football
3. Lacrosse
4. Boxing
5. Soccer
6. Baseball
7. Volleyball
8. Basketball
9. Hockey
10. Tennis
Mystery word = Stanley Cup

Lost Letters (page 8)
The missing letters spell MR DRESSUP

Round and Round (page 9)

A	T	L	A	N	T	I	C
E	S	T	R	A	I	N	E
H	R	G	Y	U	K	U	B
C	E	L	E	Y	O	I	E
R	N	N	S	E	N	T	R
O	E	A	T	S	E	C	G
R	V	E	S	E	E	H	O
R	E	B	M	E	M	D	L

Your Choice (pages 10 & 11)
1) b
2) a
3) b
4) c
5) c
6) a
7) c

Record-Makers (page 12)
1) Mike Weir
2) Clara Hughes
3) Roland Green
4) Alexandre Despatie
5) Beckie Scott
6) Christine Sinclair

Sad, Grouchy and Worthless! (page 13)
The leftover letters spell Happy Adventure, NL

Dream Teams (page 14)

Dawson City Sumos and Iqaluit Iceslingers are fake.

Calgary Storm: A-League Soccer;

Erie Otters: Ontario Hockey League;

Halifax Moosehead: Quebec Major Junior Hockey League;

Montreal Express: National Lacrosse League;

Ottawa Renegades: Canadian Football League;

Ste-Julie Panthers: National Women's Hockey League.

Juggling Jugglers (page 14)

1 & 5 are the same.

Puzzling Letters #1 (page 15)

a) quill

b) core

c) sled

d) IOU

Mystery word: Cirque du Soleil

Swim, Run & Fly (pages 16 & 17)

The made-up name is Iceflier.

Spot the Difference: Skateboard (pages 18 & 19)

(in no particular order)

- frown on skateboard graphics
- open polka dots on flag
- reversed R in PARK
- no spot on dog
- telescope on building
- skate park rules: buckle up
- 52 not 57 foreground shirt
- peace sign on middleground skateboard
- snake not dragon on skateboard
- no wheels on middleground skateboard
- backwards ballcap on sitting boy
- zigzag sock on middleground skater
- long pants on background boy
- no pole tops on city park sign

- wheel missing, foreground skateboard
- bare feet on sitting boy
- different logo on girl's t-shirt
- pattern reversed on middleground skateboard
- bird has black beak
- t-shirt logo on background watching girl

Wild Canada (page 20)

Petunia, phlox, peony, Pansy, poppy, primrose

Famous Canadians (page 21)
Craig Keilburger: youth activist, Free the Children founder
Cindy Klassen: 2003 World Champion, long track speed skating
Jennifer Robinson: six-time Canadian Figure Skating Champion
Jordin Tootoo: star junior hockey player from Rankin Inlet
Jann Arden: singer song-writer and former video-store clerk
Joel Wapnick: World Scrabble Champion 1999
Ron MacLean: TV sports host and amateur referee
Jian Ghomeshi: musician, writer and TV host
Calixa Lavallee: writer of O Canada in 1880
Gordon Korman: author of *Everest* and *Macdonald Hall* series
Chantal Kreviazuk: pop singer and student of classical piano
Moses Znaimer: TV creator of Muchmusic and other shows
Birute Galdikas: world-renowed orangutan expert

The Cars (pages 22 & 23)
His car is #3, license plate 6749

Weather Wonders (pages 24 & 25)
1) a: In winter the rivers freeze with ice at least a metre thick; this is strong enough for even heavy trucks. The Highways Departments keep the roads clear and they usually last from December to April.
2) c: and July 17th is the warmest day on average.
3) b
4) True; it is the 4th cloudiest in the world.
5) a
6) False; it's known as calving.
7) b
8) c: Over 50,000 birders from across North America participate in the annual Christmas Bird Count. If you're interested in helping contact your local birdwatching or naturalist club.

Boggling Letters (page 26)
We found 41 words:

elfin	feel	fell	fellow
fine	fink	file	fill
flew	flow	flown	foil
keep	keen	kiln	knee
knell	knife	knoll	know
leek	life	lily	line
link	lone	lonely	lowly
none	oily	week	weekly
well	wife	will	wine
wink	wolf	wonky	yell
yellow			

Good Sports (pages 27 & 28)
1) a
2) d
3) c
4) a
5) d
6) b
7) a
8) c

Eureka! (page 29)
The leftover letters spell Five Pin Bowling

Canadiana (pages 30 & 31)

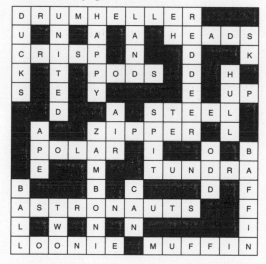

Dumb Laws (pages 32 & 33)
4 and #7 are fake

Musical Mix-Up (page 34)
Rascal2, Crazy World
The Tragically Hip, It's A Good Life If You
    Don't Weaken
Sarah Harmer, Don't Get Your Back Up
K-Os, Heaven Only Knows
David Usher, My Way Out
Barenaked Ladies, Pinch Me
Nelly Furtado, On The Radio
Sum 41, Still Waiting
Our Lady Peace, Somewhere Out There
Nickleback, How You Remind Me
Avril Lavigne, Complicated
Alanis Morissette, Hands Clean

Money Problems (page 35)
1) b
2) 1 quarter, 2 dimes and 2 nickels
3) c; if you have 3/5 of the original bill it's
worth $20; 2/5 to 3/5 is worth $10; less than
2/5 and it's worth nothing.
4) a
5) c

What's My Sport? (pages 36 & 37)
1) Field lacrosse (lacrosse)
2) Squash
3) Trampolining

Highland Dancers (page 37)
4 & 5 are the same

Giant Statues (page 38)

Tin Soldier: New Westminster, BC *9.8 metres high*

Easter Egg: Vegreville, AB *9.4 m. high*

Hockey Cards: Kelvington, SK *2.4 m. high*

Mosquito carrying a man: Upsala, ON *4.6 m. wingspan*

Camel: Glenboro, MB *7 m. high*

Milk Bottle: Montreal, QC *9.8 m. high*

Mastodon: Stewiacke, NS *4.5 m. high*

Lumberjack: Kedgwick, NB *7.6 m. high*

Fiddle: Cavendish, PE *7.4 m. high*

Moose: Goobies, NL *3.5 m. high*

Lost Letters #2 (page 39)

The missing letters spell DINOSAUR

Common Ground (pages 40 & 41)

1) a
2) a
3) b
4) a
5) c
6) c
7) b
8) b
9) c

What Am I? (pages 42 & 43)

1) Gold Rush
2) Canadarm
3) Hudson Bay

Puzzling Letters #2 (page 44)

a) night
b) ore
c) throne
d) list
Mystery word = Northern Lights

Wild Canada #2 (page 45)

Salmon, sculpin, sole, stingray, sturgeon, swordfish

Famous First Words (page 46)

1) The Day Niagara Falls Ran Dry, *David Phillips*

2) The Screech Owls' Northern Adventure, *Roy MacGregor*

3) Love You Forever, *Robert Munsch*

4) The Secret World of Og, *Pierre Berton*

5) Sunwing, *Kenneth Oppel*

6) Wow Canada! *Vivien Bowers*

7) Emily Carr Mystery, *Eric Wilson*

8) The Hockey Sweater, *Roch Carrier*

9) Jelly Belly, *Dennis Lee*

Rainbow Country (page 47)

1) Red Green
2) Orangeville
3) Red River
4) Green garbage bags
5) Blue Rodeo
6) Bluenose
7) Whitehorse
8) Black Creek
9) Pink flamingos
10) Greenpeace

Spot the Difference: Winter (pages 48 & 49)

(*in no particular order*)

• rabbits
• loops on toboggan string
• scarf on dog
• bare hand on girl falling off GT
• no hat on GT hotdogger
• upside-down maple leaf on snowboard
• missing ski on GT
• buttons on snowman
• sun-flyer, not sno-flyer
• extra tree in background

(*continued on page 69*)

Spot the Difference: Winter
(continued)

- wagon, not sled
- moon, not sun
- tassel on mitt
- circle on snowboarder hat
- surfboard, not toboggan in far background
- cap on snowman
- pompom on hat of GT girl
- number of birds
- bare foot in snowbank
- number of kids in snowball fight

Body Parts (page 52)
The leftover letters spell Skeleton Valley NU

Action Canada (pages 50 & 51)

More Choices (pages 53 & 54)
1) c
2) b
3) a
4) a
5) b
6) c
7) b
8) a
9) c

Where Am I? (page 55)
1) British Columbia
2) Nova Scotia
3) Manitoba
4) Prince Edward Island
5) Newfoundland and Labrador
6) Saskatchewan
7) Northwest Territories

Across Canada (pages 56 & 57)

Who Am I? (pages 58 & 59)
1) Marc Gagnon
2) Avril Lavigne
3) Mr. Dressup or Ernie Coombs

Confused Rivers (page 60)
1) Fraser
2) Churchill
3) Severn
4) Red
5) Peace
6) Saguenay
7) McKenzie
8) Columbia
The extra letters spell Voyageur

Odd One Out (page 61)
VJs = Red 1
World Records = world's heaviest single-day snowfall
Politicians = Robert Munsch
Comedians = Adrienne Clarkson
Bands = Missing Link
Actors = Justin Trudeau
Newfoundland Place Names = Fogarty's Cove
Athletes = Hazel Mae

You're a What? (page 62)
1) a
2) c
3) a
4) a
5) c
6) b
7) c

Round and Round Again (page 63)

K	L	O	N	D	I	K	E
E	R	S	L	E	E	T	L
T	D	E	A	D	I	O	P
T	A	I	N	B	S	Q	I
E	R	A	W	O	C	U	L
L	A	R	E	V	O	E	O
W	P	M	A	T	S	A	T
O	L	L	E	Y	R	E	T

About the Authors

Jesse Ross, co-author of the *Amazing Allstar Hockey Activity Book*, is a 16-year-old sports enthusiast and aspiring writer. **Ruth Porter**, Jesse's mom, publishes and edits the *Polestar Family Calendar*. They live in BC's Slocan Valley.

They can be contacted at njr@netidea.com

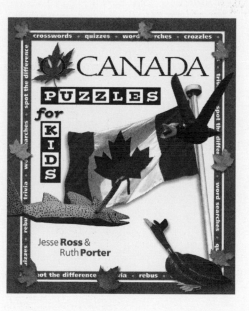

Book 1